10,000 Words: How to Increase Your Writing Speed, Build Your Confidence, and Find Your Voice

ALEX MATSUO

DEDICATION

This book is dedicated to everyone who is trying to find their voice, and make it heard. For the dreamers, the believers, the wishers, and the go-getters. For those who still yearn for something more and for a change in their life. May this book help you find your words and heighten your voice. You have a story that the world wants to hear!

CONTENTS

ACKNOWLEDGMENTS

I would like to thank all of my friends and family who have come together this past year to uplift me and support me in my times of trial. I could not have survived 2014 without you!   Special thanks to my mother, my Uncle Jon, as well as my friends in a certain cast of characters that include a dear elephant and a bird with a one-feathered tail. This kangaroo thanks you!

INTRODUCTION

You may be thinking: Why I am writing this book?

Well, let me ask you a question in return, dear reader.

How many times have we been in a situation where we were pressed for time and needed to write a large amount of words in a matter of a day or two? Whether you have a paper for school, a major project for work, or you just have a compelling story to tell and you need to write it down before the idea is lost, the thought of writing 10,000 words a day is overwhelming. When I was in this situation, I had no resources to seek out besides a few eBooks online and a blog post or two, but I couldn't relate to any of the information. This is by no means an attempt to disregard or trivialize the other fantastic books out there on a similar subject. In fact, they are great sources of information. But when it came to writing 10,000 words in a day, I hadn't found something that worked for me and my process of writing.

When I first started writing, my process was to just get it all out on paper, and then *maybe* I would go back and edit. But, in reality, I wasn't confident in my writing abilities, so going back for editing was embarrassing for me. I didn't want to go back and read how bad my paper was. It was a shameful and embarrassing process for me. So I played with fate and turned in my work to my professors and hoped for the best. Sometimes my work was praised and given full credit. Other times, I had to rewrite parts before my final grade was given.

In this time of my life, specifically school, writing was not a positive outlet for me. I dreaded writing assignments. But where did this disdain come from? All of my life, I struggled with writing. My essays in high school were atrocious. I never wrote for pleasure, and I didn't even write in a diary.

But I was very creative. Every day, I played out stories and fantasies in my head. From hypothetical "what if" situations to simple daydreaming, I always had something going on in my head. My creative outlet at the time was theatre. I would perform and say the lines. That was my outlet for all the creativity in my head. I even read like a bookworm, often getting out one to two books per week while still in high school.

Then, sometime in my mid-twenties, that changed. Specifically, graduate school changed my perception. I was no longer confined to the boundaries of general education. But instead, I was assigned to write about my passions and what I believed in. For the first time in my life, writing was an enjoyable venture that would continue through beyond my graduation day.

So what changed?

The content changed.

My attitude changed.

This ended up being my breakthrough when it came to my writing. It was then that I realized that writing was an extension of myself, putting my thoughts to paper, thus giving it immortality in some form.

You're probably reading this book so that you can figure out how to write a large amount of words per day, or to even get over a writer's block. While there is no magic or "quick & easy" solution, I can give you the tips and tricks that helped me finish some of my largest writing projects. My goal is for this book to become a resource for you and your writing goals.

Since you're trying to write faster, it will be safe for me to assume that you would like to read and finish this book quickly so you can get to work. This is why, ironically, I've made this book about 10,000 words, give or take an extra thousand words. You don't even need to read it in a linear context, but instead, go to the chapter with the topic that you're need of the most support.

If you find this book useful, and/or you enjoy it, please do not hesitate to recommend it and spread the word to your friends and family. Even leaving a review online can make the difference between someone changing the course of their writing career forever.

So, curl up. Grab a hot cup of tea and some chocolate, get ready to start the course of changing your writing skills, and how you express yourself for the rest of your life.

Cheers.

WHAT IS WRITING?

If you were to go on the computer and search for the definition of writing, you'll get a range of philosophical answers such as, "Expressing the human soul" to more literal and technical answers such as "A series of cohesive patterns using letters and numbers to present a thought." Of course, I'm just summing up assumed answers, but the actual findings would be similar. For millions of years (yes millions), humans have been expressing ourselves using an outside source besides what our physical body can communicate with our voices and gestures.

From cave paintings to calligraphy, we have found a way to communicate our needs, thoughts, and feelings on different venues such as walls, clothing, skin, and paper. For our pen, we have used paint, water, oil, and blood. Simply put, writing is an important part of not only our history, but also our present and future. If it wasn't important, the practice would have fallen to the wayside centuries ago.

If you look over writing samples from the greatest authors of our history, you can see the evolution of our existence. But it is also important to look at the writings of common folk, the people who lived their ordinary lives without fame or fortune. In fact, these writings are probably even more important than the celebrities of the time. There, you can see where we were as a society, how an educated person wrote, and what the writings of an uneducated person was like...if they could write at all. Even to this day, there are people who don't know how to read and write, and that truly is a *tragedy*. So, the fact that you have the ability to read this book to assist with your writing skills is truly a blessing alone. Take a moment to marinate in that.

Simply put, writing is a form of communication. It is the opportunity to express what is in our minds. In the academic context, it is a chance to prove that we understand the material being taught and we know how to apply it to our work and study. In terms of writing fiction, it is a chance to tell the stories of the imaginary world in our heads. When it comes to writing non-fiction, it is our chance to make a stand about our knowledge and explore new ideas and theories about one of the thousands of topics out there.

But in its very essence, writing is the opportunity to change a life. When soldiers were dying on the battlefield, if they were able to do it themselves, they wrote letters to their loved ones and telling them how much they meant to them. If they couldn't write, someone else was there to transcribe. For those who have survived the horrors of human existence, writing told their stories so that history wouldn't repeat itself. In all of the craziness of life, writing will continue to survive, from the dragging of the quill to the typing on the keyboard.

Here we come to the very essence of the book; writing is important. It is because of this importance that we struggle so much with writing. Our intelligence is graded based on our ability to write. This is something that will always remain true even after we have earned our certificates and degrees. If you can write well, you are in a good place to find a decent job. Having the ability to clearly communicate thoughts and ideas opens a world of opportunity for the good writer.

There have been countless books written when it comes to improving grammar, spelling, and conveying points and ideas. People have made thousands of dollars with workshops, seminars, and more. Writing has become a multi-billion dollar industry from word processing programs, editing services, people being paid to write papers on another's behalf, plagiarism, and publishing. If you can do more than just write, but also edit, then that is another career opportunity if you have the patience and the skill to pay attention to detail.

The reason why I'm going over this, my dear reader, is so that you can understand why I've become so passionate about writing. It is not even due to the practice of writing itself, but the very role it has played in the survival of our society and humanity. If writing did not exist, we would not exist or survive as a society.

Not only is it important, it is a basic part of our life.

But again, it is something that most people struggle with. Why?

The fact of the matter is it's because we don't write enough. Even if we're in school, we only write when we are asked to. After the education chapter of our lives is over, what happens next? Writing is something that is becoming a bit of a dying art form. Even, with the innovation of the Internet and stories being told with a click of a picture, writing isn't a part of regular life anymore. The more we are distanced from writing, the harder it is to get back into.

For example, let's consider the time before computers and the internet were the mainstream. People wrote letters to each other on a daily basis. Penmanship was a highly valued skill, and the ability to put your words together was the norm. If you read the letters of Civil War soldiers, you will see alliteration, personification, and overall, beautiful writing. This trend continued until technology began to play an invasive and necessary part of our lives. With the invention of the telephone, letters were no longer needed as much because it wasn't the sole form of communication. With the invention of the computer, ideas could be expressed, written down, and delivered at a faster pace. With the invention of the internet, and texting, quality of writing began to decline in the conventional popular as words are condensed to just a few letters. Speed began to take a priority over quality, for the sake of getting a message out as soon as possible.

I think the concept of "speed over quality", plus the two extremes of writing with all emotion with no objective versus the disassociation of emotions with a lost objective, has contributed to our fears when it comes to writing, especially if you're writing for a project or a class assignment. If it is something you are forced to do, any time that is dedicated to the project will feel like it is going by slowly and it is time wasted.

It is time to change that perception of writing.

WHY ARE YOU WRITING?

There are a multitude of reasons why you may be writing. You might be doing a daily journal of your life, you might be trying to work through an emotional time, you're trying to get that book out (finally), you might be writing for a school assignment, or you could be writing for work. When it comes to reasons for writing, the possibilities are endless.

Whatever your reason for writing, the biggest challenge is to sit down and get started. Just like the anticipation of a scary experience is worse than the actual ride, I find that once I'm rolling, the writing process is much easier. However, just getting started can be so difficult sometimes! How do we exactly start on this journey?

Well we have to figure out why we're even bothering to write in the first place.

The biggest hurdle we need to overcome is figuring out and making peace with why we are writing. Believe it or not, this is a crucial step to figure out and realize before you start writing *anything*. This needs to be done because figuring out why you're writing sets a solid foundation for the rest of your journey. Look at it this way; if you don't know why you're writing, you're not going to accomplish much. Most people don't go traveling without a purpose, or start their work day with an objective.

If you're writing for school, the completion of this assignment will go towards your grade. Instead of keeping this immediate assignment in mind, think further ahead. Before you begin, mentally prepare yourself:

1. Close your eyes
2. Take five deep breaths.
3. As you breathe, visualize yourself writing the assignment with ease.
4. Visualize your fingers typing ferociously and the words just coming out of your mind and into your fingers.
5. In your own words, say to yourself that you are knowledgeable in the topic you're writing about, and that what you have to say has value.
6. Picture yourself successfully completing the assignment.
7. Picture your teacher, professor, TA, GA, whoever is grading your assignment. Visualize them being overly satisfied with your work and giving you full credit or a high letter grade.

8.   Take a few more deep breaths, and open your eyes when you're ready.

Practice this a few times before you begin writing. While it may seem silly, if you are not confident in your writing abilities, this will set the right tone before you embark on this task. I feel confident enough in saying that the majority of the time, writing is a mental game with confidence, and you have to decide if it's on your team or not. If you are confident, the words will flow. If you are not confident, you will get stuck, and eventually frustrated.

For most academic writing assignments, you're trying to show that you have retained and applied the knowledge that your teacher has taught you. It is showing that you have, indeed, learned something. Writing assignments are a chance to demonstrate your understanding of the subject. As a former graduate assistant, I tended to give more points to the students who not only applied the subjects that were taught, but showed me how they applied it to their personal lives, or used comparisons and examples to make their point. Most students will just reiterate and regurgitate what their teacher said in class. While that is still acceptable, it is a bit dry, and more often than not, it will result in an average grade. Shoot for the stars! These are your grades we're talking about!

If you are writing for work, the exercise above will be beneficial as well. It will just need a few tweaks to better fit your situation. Regardless of your beliefs, putting a positive image of your work being well-received out there into the universe is never a bad thing. Positive begets positive, negative begets negative.

Now, if you are writing for more personal reasons, you have to find your motivation. With personal assignments, it can be easy to procrastinate and put the project on the back burner. Once you find out why you're writing, you're halfway there on getting your motivation. If you need something motivate you quickly without exercises or thought, give yourself a deadline. Or, fate could be giving you a deadline. For example, when I realized that my elderly relatives were passing on, I wanted to write and get their stories down before it was too late. Hopefully, your motivation isn't quite as dramatic as mine was.

One of the hardest things to do on a personal writing project is getting started and sticking with it. If you're not motivated to complete the project, you may need to rethink the angle in which you are approaching this. I would say about 80% of the writing battle is *motivation*. It won't get done unless you have something driving you to do it. With school, or work, the motivation is easy because someone else is dependent on the assignment being completed, or grades are hanging on the line. With personal writing, such as journaling, writing fiction or non-fiction, it's not so easy.

However, you can use a similar visual that I presented at the beginning of the chapter. This will be effective, especially if you're hoping to publish or self-publish your work. How often do we start something and then put it on the back burner indefinitely?

Essentially, what I want you to take away from this chapter is to work out *why* you are writing. While it may seem trivial or basic, it will help you in your journey, and most importantly, it will help you persevere when you're dealing with stamina issues or writer's block.

Another way to help you realize your reason and motivation for writing is to change your attitude about the task. This doesn't necessarily mean that you're approaching the assignment with negativity, but attitude has a lot to do with our perception of writing. If we have a casual or non-urgent attitude, procrastination sets in. If we are emotionally detached from writing, we tend to lose our "why" in the reason we're writing in the first place. So, keep your attitude in check, and look into yourself often. This "why" segment isn't exclusive to the beginning of the journey. In fact, I recommend checking in with yourself often, especially in times of writer's block.

Once you have mastered and worked through why you are writing during this session, it is time to begin.

BUILDING STAMINA

Here we approach probably one of the most useful chapters in this book. No matter where your skill level is at, building writing stamina is something that we can all improve on, even myself. Stamina essentially means how long you're able to write without stopping. Just as when an athlete is trying to build their stamina, they can't run a marathon on their first day of training. It takes a gradual build-up that is heading towards success. If you try to do too much too soon, you'll experience burnout and won't want to try again.

Depending on how much time you have, you can gradually build up your stamina with daily writing exercises. If you're pressed for time, not all hope is lost. This chapter will offer some insight on how to start writing for longer sprints, as well as increasing your typing speed. Then, you'll have speed *and* longevity, which are fantastic tools to have in your writing career.

First thing you need to figure out is exactly how much time you can devote each day to writing. If you have five minutes, fifteen minutes, thirty minutes, or an hour to spare, use the time you have wisely. To start, we will go about this as if you have only a few minutes a day, and you're trying to increase your stamina so that you can handle your longer writing projects at work that have a time crunch.

If you want to figure out how many words you can type in a minute, there are numerous online programs where you can test this. One option is that you can set up a timer for a minute and start writing a list of pre-selected words, or you can use one of the exercises in this book and go for a minute and see how far you get. Typing with the intention of speed will produce interesting results, and will help you figure out what kind of goal you want to set. Once you have an idea of where you're at in terms of speed, then you can focus on your *longevity*.

To figure out is where you are at in terms of your stamina right now, set a stopwatch and start writing something that interests you (we'll discuss topics in just a moment). Once you start feeling like you're ready to stop, go ahead and stop your watch. The time listed is your starting time for stamina. There are a variety of reasons to stop. It could be attention span, fatigue, eye or hand pain, etc. Go ahead and count it. You want to get a baseline on where you're starting so you can track your progress. I like to keep track of my speed and longevity with a spreadsheet program, but writing it down on paper with a date and minutes and hour (if applicable) is good too.

I recommend reading each exercise before doing it, so that you don't need to stop and waste time checking the directions. For this exercise, pick a topic of interest. It doesn't even need to make sense. The topic we'll use for this example is your dream from the previous night.

1. Start with the first thing you remember from the dream and start typing with a linear timeline to the best of your abilities. Don't worry about grammar or punctuation.
2. What happened in the beginning? Write it. Don't worry about details, just get it out. We'll fill in the details later.
3. What happened in the middle? Write it. Again, do not worry about the details.
4. What happened in the end? Write it. Just the basics.
5. Take a step back and admire the words you put down.

Now, you have a skeleton to work with. You'll probably have about 50-100 words typed out. If you feel energized and like you can do more, keep going on to the second half of this exercise.

6. Fill in the details in the beginning of your dream: Who was there? Do you know them? What do they look like? Why do you think they were there?
7. Fill in the details about the middle of your dream: Did some accident happen? Were you trying to solve a problem? Were you searching for something?
8. Fill in the details about the end of your dream: Did the issue get resolved? Was there any conflict at all? Would you consider this a good dream or a bad dream?
9. If you can't remember the details listed above, then make them up! This exercise can also get you started on your creative juices.
10. Take a step back and admire your updated work.

Congratulations, you just wrote out a story! At this point, you have probably written anywhere between 200 and 500 words. Maybe even more if you remember the details of your dream or you decided to get creative and add some additional details from your own creative mind. This little exercise is just for you. You won't be able to build your stamina if you don't enjoy what you're doing. I find that writing out my dreams is a great little writing "workout" to keep myself tuned up. Don't worry about grammar too much when you're first starting out. The point is to build your stamina and be able to write more words in a single session. If you desire to do so, go back and fix your grammar afterward.

If you don't want to write about your dreams, then you can write about other topics of your life. Here is a list of random topics to help get you started:

- What you ate for lunch
- A trip to the mall
- A conversation you had with a friend or family member
- Making up what you think your pet does all day while you're at work.
- Talking about a day where you got stuck in traffic
- What would you do if you could fly
- Step-by-step process of how you made dinner
- A day in the life of an alien
- How to make the perfect sandwich
- Describing your last trip

As you can see, these topics are not very deep, and perhaps a little esoteric as well. What I am hoping this shows you is that, when it comes to increasing your stamina, all you need to do is *write*. Write about anything that comes to your mind that you're interested in. As I said before, it doesn't even have to make much sense because it is only your eyes that are gazing upon these words. Hopefully, this will relieve some performance pressure as well.

If you're desiring an exercise topic that will help gauge your emotional writing, here are some topics to consider:

- Describing the last day with your loved one before they died.
- Going over a fight that changed your relationship.
- Moment-by-moment recap of the birth of your children, grandchildren, etc.
- The moment you realized that you were no longer a child.
- Writing about someone or something that broke your heart.
- Realizing it was time to say goodbye to your pet.
- A fight against a debilitating or terminal disease.

I'm not a psychologist or a psychiatrist, so approach these topics with caution. When it comes to emotional writing, there's a good chance that these topics could either reopen or rub salt into old wounds, or they could even help you deal and work through unresolved issues. Before embarking on this particular exercise, be sure to consult with a licensed professional.

There is no doubt that emotional writing can get a large amount of words out in a short amount of time. I will tend to use writing as my own therapy when dealing through an issue in my life. You know the classic dealing of writing a letter to someone that you'll never send? There's something to that. In this case, you are also integrating writing into more areas of your life, thus, you'll start writing more often.

I do want to make a final note on grammar. Earlier in the chapter, I expressed to not be concern with it as you're building your stamina. I stand by this, as the exercises are there to help you write longer and faster. Should you decide that you like the fruit of your work, be sure to go back and do some editing so that it is reader-friendly to your intended audience.

Overall, what I want you to get out of this chapter is to start small and grow. If you try too much at once, you'll eventually become frustrated and not want to write much in the future. But, I promise you, you'll improve with each session. Building your stamina and longevity should be an enjoyable experience, so that you'll *want* to do it! The more you write, the better you'll get. Then, once you have to write for work or school, you'll have worked on your stamina to the point where you'll be ready to tackle on any task with a focused mind.

FINDING YOUR VOICE

With so much information out there in the world today that is still being explored, it's inevitable that numerous people will write on the same subjects. If we all wrote in the exact same way, not only would it be boring, but it would also be a form of copying and plagiarism. As we are all unique individuals, our writing is unique as well. No one else writes in the exact same style as you do, and you don't write exactly like anyone else. Sure, there are different styles that we might admire, but our writing style, or our "voice" derives from our own minds, and it is the patterns and the "firing" inside our brain that cooks up our writing voice. With each style, diction plays a role as it determines our word choice and whether we use positive or negative connotations (otherwise how we spin our sentences).

There are the basics in terms of voices. First, there is the **narrative** style of writing, which is telling a story and your audience is expected to learn some sort of lesson from it. Then there are the three different perspectives of the writing, including first, second, and third person. **First person** uses the "I" and "we" pronouns. **Second person** addresses the reader by using variations of the "you" pronoun. For example, this book uses second person often because I am talking directly to you, reader. Third person is the style most commonly used in fiction and academic writing by using the pronouns, "she", "he", and "it." Mixing up the use of these pronouns will often lead to confusion, so be careful when using first, second, or third person, and watch your transitions.

The next step that you need to take is figure out exactly what your *tone* of voice is. As we established our baseline writing stamina, we need to establish our baseline "writing tone" and work from there. Some people may start off writing in a very formal tone, while most others will start off with a casual or informal tone. From there, our tone can be molded and shaped for each writing project that we take on. The best way to figure out our baseline is to read emails, messages, and previous papers. We can establish our starting point by looking at our previous work. The reason why I don't recommend doing an exercise is due to the fact that you'd be walking into the assessment already aware of what you're measuring, and your results would be tainted. So, take a look at your previous work and we will go from there.

In order to work on our voice and style, we need to explore the different categories of tone.

The first category is the **informal tone**. The informal tone is very casual. It is the same kind of tone you would use with your friends and family, in a non-professional environment. Numerous blogs and social media posts will be done in an informal voice. You will usually use this voice for when you are expressing your beliefs, concerns, commentary, ideas, and more. There is no pressure to really impress anyone with big words or a solid grammatical structure. I actually enjoy reading material in an informal tone because it gives me the opportunity to take a visit into the mind of the individual, and I find it more relatable. I feel you can also get to know someone rather intimately by reading their informal tone. You can actually get an idea of their academic background, personality, and mental state by reading the informal tone.

The second category is the **formal tone**. This is the tone you'll read in a work or academic setting. You will use this when addressing your coworker, boss, professor, and anywhere else where your professionalism may be judged. People will often write with a formal tone for when they want to be taken seriously, and be heard by a more influential and powerful audience. If it sounds judgmental, well, that's because it is. You wouldn't write to your boss or teacher in the same voice that you would address your best friend (unless you have a formal relationship with them). Your words are chosen carefully, and the way you structure your thoughts are exceptionally important in order to communicate your thoughts and ideas properly.

The overall **tone** can speak volumes about a writer's background. When I use the word, "tone", I essentially mean the attitude of the voice. You can also judge originality, authenticity, and personality based on the writer's voice. We can look at these areas as subcategories.

When it comes to **originality**, if the writer is well-versed in their topic, then the majority of their ideas will be original since there has been time to "marinate" so to speak in the concept and come up with their own beliefs.

When it comes to **authenticity**, you can also read how authentic a writer is based on their convictions in their writing. When someone is writing something that they care about, there will be an underlying drive and passion in their voice. If the writer cares, then the reader will care. You can usually tell if the writer cares about their work or not based on their journey throughout the piece, and how well they maintain their thoughts in the structure. When a writer cares, there is authenticity, and you tend to better believe their argument.

Now, here we are at **personality**. This can also go hand-in-hand with what was said in the previous paragraph. Personality isn't just reserved for the informal voice. Just as you change your personality and actions based on your external environment, you can still project your personality in formal writing.

Overall, writing is the expression of your thoughts and ideas. How you express what's in your mind will vary based on different contexts of your life. Finding your voice doesn't mean that you'll be using just one, but instead, multiple voices. But, in whatever you do, don't lose what makes you. Whether you're writing academically or a casual email, you have a shining personality to translate into words, and it will make you stand out above the rest of your friends, class or workplace.

In a public setting, be very careful with how you use your writing voice. With social media on the rise, and blogs being maintained on a regular basis, your voice can be judged by future academic institutions, employers, dates, the possibilities are endless. You want your voice to reflect the value that is inside of you, and it is never too late to start creating a presence for yourself using your words. The more you practice this in your personal life, the easier it will translate over to your writing where your professionalism, or at least your grades, will be affected.

DEALING WITH WRITER'S BLOCK

Probably one of the most common issues we run into when it comes to writing is the dreaded *writer's block*, meaning that the words we want to say won't come out. We don't know where to begin, where to continue, or where to end. It is a frustrating moment that can either make or break our writing. It is a very common dilemma that hits nearly every person, whether they consider themselves to be writers or not. What is probably terrifying is that there isn't just one type of writer's block. There are indeed different varieties of this demon, and if you want to overcome it, you have to know your enemy inside and out. This means knowing *why* you are experiencing this kind of writer's block. Once you accomplish that, you can plan your counter-attack and get over the writer's block hurdle sooner and get back to writing.

You Can't Begin: This is the most common type of writer's block that spans across the genres. From academic, to professional, to creative writing, starting the project can be the biggest challenge. The easy and less knowledgeable answer would be to just start. But this remedy just isn't the case when you're staring at a blank screen. You're probably feeling overwhelmed, and set really high standards for yourself. Or, if this is an assignment, you're probably feeling confused by the prompt and not sure what to make of it.

The best way to combat this type of writer's block is to make an outline. Before you begin, map out you are going to write about. If you're writing a paper for school, chances are you probably have an outline already. If you don't, make one. Work out what you're going to say in the beginning, the middle (or your points), and the end. If you go in already thinking about your topic at hand, then once you start, you'll already have it in your brain. I tend to make little short bullet points that I can expand on once I start writing. When you don't know where to begin, create a map.

The Ideas Are Messy: This is a situation where you actually have a plethora of ideas, but you can't work them out on paper. Again, this can be very common with creative writers as well as academic writers. The best thing to do in this situation is micro-managing. Write a paragraph or so on each idea, and see which one can be expanded. It's a bit more of an expanded version of an outline, but not quite so structure.

I like to put a sentence or two summing up the idea, and then a paragraph expanding on it. With this, you'll figure out what ideas are worth keeping and what ideas aren't so great. To be honest, if an idea is bad, there is no salvaging it. Forcing more words than necessary on an idea is a form of torture for not only yourself, but also the reader, and should be scrapped immediately. As mentioned before, pursue the idea that gives you the most inspiration and excitement so you'll be able to write more.

Stuck In the Middle: This is a common dilemma a lot of writers face. The day before, the ideas were flowing, things were happening. But then day two rolls around and now you're facing a blank sheet of paper, unsure of what to do next. What has worked for me in the past is to take a short break from the paper and focus on another topic. You can use the same characters and idea, or you can start something completely out in left field. If I try to force an idea out that doesn't exist, I'll end up creating more useless words that will get me frustrated. But sometimes, taking an unexpected turn will do you good to get things moving again. If you're working on an essay, bring up a totally random point to connect with the rest of your text later. Even if you don't keep it, chances are your creative juices will be flowing again. The same goes for creative writing. Make your characters do something completely random and unexpected to get the plot moving again. The twists and turns you put yourself through might just help you find your path again. Some of the greatest classics were created because the author took an unexpected turn in the plot.

The scenarios I listed above aren't the only situations you'll run into as a writer. The best thing I can tell you is that when you get stuck with a writer's block, *do not despair.* It is a completely normal part of the writing process. How you handle the block will help you not only in your writing, but in your problem solving skills in general. If you reach a block where all hope is lost, take a break from the project, if time allows. Taking a break will help you breathe new life into your ideas. The most important thing to remember is to not walk away from writing because of a block. Keep writing, even if you have to work on something else. Sometimes, even working on another chapter or assignment will inspire something for what I originally walked away from. And that is a fantastic dilemma to be in, having to switch back and forth between the chapters.

During my most intense blocks, sometimes I'll use one of the exercises from the stamina chapter and that will help me come up with new ideas. It is also important to not stop writing. Just as an athlete may run into bad training sessions or poor results from competitions, they don't stop working. If you walk away from writing, you will start to lose your flow, and once the flow is interrupted, it is even harder to get it going again.

Of course, this will all depend on what you're working on. If it's an academic or work-related assignment, you have no choice but to continue working on the project if you are to complete it (and then you might walk away). If the project is a personal one, then I must stress even more to not walk away or take too long of a break. How many people have writing projects, such as plays, biographies, memoirs, creative writing, etc. tucked away into their computers, collecting dust? With deadlines, there is motivation. But as we also know, deadlines can be the culprit of writer's block.

I realize that this chapter may not have been the most helpful in terms of a "quick fix" for writer's block. The techniques above have worked for me in different scenarios, and hopefully they can help you as well. Writer's block has been an intriguing topic for many, and entire books have been written dedicated to the subject with numerous exercises, tips, and advice to help readers combat the issue. Please, do not give up if you encounter writer's block. Know that it is a normal thing to go through, and some of humanity's greatest authors and playwrights have dealt with it. I feel that writer's block is one of those tests that keep coming back to check our passion as well as our skill. Remember the reason you are writing in the first place, and may that give you what you need to persevere through the trench.

WRITING ACCOUNTABILITY

When it comes to furthering our writing career, a vital step to improving our work is having some sort of accountability. This begins with the practice of writing every day.

At first glance, the idea of dedicating a chapter to writing everyday can seem like it's a bit of a stretch. But, whether you realize it or not, you write every day of your life. It could be a text message, an email, a post on social media, or a blog post. It is writing, even if it is for a moment. The reason why we write so much is because it is a part of how we communicate. Those who don't have the words to verbally speak can put them down on paper. History has been recorded through writing. It is one of the most vital communication tools every day that we use as often as we talk, if not more.

Once we acknowledge that we write on a daily basis, it can be easier to acknowledge that we need to write in some form as much as possible if we want to improve this practice. Of course, this needs to remain an enjoyable part of our routine. Topics can include a recap of your day, a thought that you have, solving a problem, or telling a funny story. It doesn't have to be written in a journal, or on a blog. It can be as easy as writing an email to yourself, or writing a note on social media.

As I've stated before in this short little eBook, the more you write, the better at it you become. Making writing a daily exercise can be an enjoyable experience, especially if you want to increase your speed, as writing on the computer every day on a keyboard can also help improve your amount of words per minute, which can be beneficial on the job front.

If you're just starting to work on your writing career, then writing each day is crucial. You'll start to become more aware of your writing style, how fast you write, and what inspires you. Also, determining what kind of writing you want to do with your career will impact what kind of writing you do each day. You want to train your brain for the appropriate genre.

For example, I mainly write non-fiction, so I do a lot of blogging and airing my thoughts on various social media outlets. I also take advantage of academic websites where I can upload my papers of various topics in relation to my fields of study.

Another way to write every day and receive more of a return is to do freelance writing. Not only do you get to write, but you can make a few dollars writing 500 words here and there. You will receive feedback from your clients, which in turn, will help you improve your writing by focusing on your weaker areas. Freelance writing also forces you to distinguish your tone and voice for each client by deciding on whether you need to write with a more professional voice, or have a more informal tone. Freelance writing taught me a lot about myself and helped me determine whether I really wanted to pursue writing as part of my career.

Writing every day can either be a private venture, or a public display. I've seen people keep a blog that they update daily with a variety of writing styles. They keep their exercises and practice sessions public for the purpose of getting constructive feedback. With the nature of the Internet, of course constructive criticism isn't always possible. Plus, you have to have a solid backbone in order to do it. Feelings can easily get hurt when you put your work out there in a public venue.

If the Internet is too overwhelming, there are writing circles in your community where you can share your work and exercises. If there isn't a group, start one. Most of these groups work as a type peer review, where you bring copies of your work and pass them around the group. This tends to be a safer environment where little to no judgment is passed. Everyone in that group is there for a reason: to improve their writing. These groups will also offer assignments with a due date (usually the meeting day), which helps with accountability and follow through.

The final way to continue writing every day is finding a trusted friend or family member to read your work. If even the group setting is too much, you can start off small with a single person who will critique you in the way that you wish. Once your confidence builds, you can move on to peer review if that is something you want to do. The reason why I keep stressing on having a second set of eyes on your work is because there are things that you won't notice about your own writing. We immediately have a bias about our own work. There could be habits or tendencies that we have and we don't notice right away.

This is all a part of having that writing accountability. But, I also understand that showing your work to someone else is a very vulnerable action, and it takes a certain amount of bravery to accomplish. If you're able to show your work to a friend, a group, or even the Internet, I applaud you. However, if you're still working on putting yourself out there, privately editing and self-critiquing is a great option too. As the old saying goes, we are own biggest critics. I do a lot of self-editing and critiquing of my own work to the point where I conjure tears. Sometimes I can be a little too hard on myself, and not give myself as much credit as others think I deserve. Sometimes that second set of eyes will assure you that you're doing just fine.

Ultimately, you need to do what works best for you. If you're serious about improving your writing, making yourself accountable is an important step towards that goal. Otherwise, you'll be trapped in a cycle of writing blind, and hoping for the best. While there are brilliant writers out there who could get away with publishing a first draft, the rest of us cannot do that. Regardless of whether you're writing for school, work, or your own projects, there is a lot of competition out there in terms of quality of writing. Accountability is a way to put your work above the rest, and constantly improve.

HOW TO WRITE 10,000 WORDS IN A DAY

Here we are at the chapter that you probably bought this book for. I was inspired to dive deeper into this concept after I found myself writing over 20,000 words in a weekend due to procrastinating over a book deadline. It was a self-published book, but I had a timeline that I wanted to stick to, and writing this massive amount of words in a matter of a day or two was a necessity. On the first day, I wrote 12,000 words, exceeding my original goal. The next day, I wrote 8,000 words. A little short of my 10,000 word goal, but it averaged out to be just fine and on track.

I'm going to be brutally honest in this chapter, because I don't want to sugarcoat this task in any way, shape, or form. If I do that, you'll be angry that the task was more difficult than you expected, or you'll accuse me of not painting a realistic picture. This chapter will be solely from my perspective. So, here we go!

In order to achieve this goal, I had to stay incredibly focused. I essentially had to unplug the television, turn off the Internet, and step away from my phone. Of course, I took breaks to sleep, go to the bathroom, eat, and stretch. If I got too distracted, I was away from my work for too long, thus, adding more time to the clock.

Also, I want to take a moment to note that you can't really accomplish this feat if you haven't been writing already. If you're attempting to do this after taking a break, or not writing at all, this task might be difficult. If you've been training, building your stamina, and practicing your writing every day, then this challenge won't quite be so overwhelming. I like to compare this task to running a marathon. The runner doesn't just get out of bed one day and just run 26.2 miles. It takes months of training for the runner to be ready. It's a test of stamina, endurance, and mental patience. The same way goes for writing 10,000 words in a day, especially if you're attempting to do this for a few days in a row.

After doing some searches on the Internet and seeing what others did to accomplish this task, I decided to just go for it and see what happens. In total, this task took me about 12-15 hours. Here are the things that helped me achieve this goal.

1. **Plan Ahead:** A few days before my writing weekend, I made a game plan. I did my research early, and wrote notes on the points I wanted to make. By doing the research before, and setting up my foundation, I didn't have to stop to do it while I was in the middle of my writing. Again, making that map for this long journey.

2. **Clear Your Calendar:** It is best to do this task on a weekend. Or, if you want to take time off of work, choose the end or the beginning of the work week so you have an extended weekend. Make sure you have no obligations on the day that you're writing. Not only does this relieve you from having to go anywhere, but it clears your mind of distractions.

3. **Create a Schedule:** If you have been working on building your writing stamina, you'll have a good idea of how many words you can type per minute and hour. For myself, I can write a good 2,000 words per hour if I have no interruptions. This is where the planning comes in. But, to be honest, you'll most likely start off fast, but that pace will not last and you will eventually slow down. Your eyes might get tired, your brain will start to get foggy, or your fingers might start hurting. You'll need to factor this in when it comes to your schedule. I would get the easier stuff typed out first while you have fresh energy, and when you start to slow down, take on the meatier parts of your writing project. Do not pressure yourself to keep your schedule linear. In fact, jumping around and going back and forth will give your brain a boost, and you might find yourself speeding up your pace. Also, factor in breaks. More on that later.

4. **What to Eat & Drink:** It is awfully tempting to stock your refrigerator with ice cream, soda, juices, energy drinks, crackers, chips, etc. since it is easy food to eat that is tasty, giving your brain those happy feelings while you're writing. The drawback of eating these kinds of foods is that it will make you tired and give you a foggy brain. When I was writing my 20,000 words, I kept a supply of fresh vegetables and fruit on hand. I liked carrots and celery because they were crunchy, and I could dip them into ranch and hummus for that extra flavor to make my brain happy. If you want to keep

your mind fresh, you'll need to keep fresh food on hand. It will keep you alert and take away that brain fog that comes with processed foods. Also, as tempting as it is to consume coffee or energy drinks, keep your beverages limited to water and iced tea. The iced tea is a personal choice since I tend to associate warm tea with bedtime. If frequent bathroom trips are a concern, train your body to take in more liquid about a week ahead of your writing day. Or, bring your laptop in the bathroom with you. Your time will definitely not be wasted.

5. **Breaks & Sleep:** Your stamina will be tested during this challenge. The next best thing you can do is take breaks, and there is no shame in this. If the number of breaks are a concern, be sure you have been working on your stamina before taking this on. Your body will tell you when you need to take a break. You will become so tired that focusing on the screen will be a challenge. Your words won't be quite so coherent. You will make mistakes often. When this occurs, you don't want to go any further. My average break time occurred about every two hours for about 15 minutes. After about four hours of writing, I took a nap. Sleeping gives your brain a chance to completely rest and recharge. Sometimes you might even get new ideas from the recharge. There is no shame in taking breaks or taking a nap for an hour (or two).

6. **When to Edit:** Since time is of the essence, and you're trying to get out a large amount of words, just type. Don't worry about the editing. After the day is done, you can go back and clean up your work when your mind is fresher. If you constantly edit as you write, you will not only be losing on precious time, but you'll wear yourself out quicker. Leave the red pen for after you're done. If you've done your research and created your outline of what you needed to get done, hopefully the editing aspect won't be too much of beast.

7. **Distractions:** You want to be able to be productive on this 10,000 word day. Therefore, you need to do what you need to do in order to make it happen. If you can't write while your house is dirty, clean it. If you need the television on while you write, turn it on. If you need the help of music to get you through, then by all means, turn on the music. If you know you'll get distracted by texts, then let your friends and family know what you're planning to do and gently inform them that your phone will be off. If you tend to be distracted by social media, then unplug the Internet and turn off your phone data. You want to create an environment that will foster creativity

and progress. Do what it takes to achieve it. This may sound like you're putting yourself in isolation. Given the weight of the task, that's what you're doing.

This is how I was able to write 20,000 words in a weekend. After I was done, I'm pretty sure I slept for about 10 hours each day, and I felt like I could take over the world.

This takes a lot of hard work and discipline. If you have been preparing by doing the exercises and taking the advice of this book, then the task is hopefully not quite so difficult. It's just a matter of applying yourself and getting it all done. Again, I won't sugar coat it and say this is the easiest thing to do. But if you apply yourself and prepare, you'll reap the rewards and be proud of yourself for accomplishing quite a feat. If this is something you want to do regularly, start with one day a week, or even a month, and build from there. You can apply these practices to virtually any writing project, and achieve great results.

GOING PUBLIC...OR PUBLISHED

One of the questions I get asked the most often is how to publish your first book. When it comes to publishing, whether it's self-publishing or being published by a major company, it is quite an accomplishment. Authors are going the self-publishing route more often these days, and I can't really say which path is better. In my opinion, I feel that being published by a company is a major achievement because it is based on another person's opinion. If they find your work to be good enough to where they're willing to invest time and money into you, then you must have some talent and even a promising writing career. It's a credibility concern for me. However, some of the best books I've ever read have been self-published, or in a venue where the author had complete control.

There are benefits to self-publishing. You can crank out books at a faster rate and put them out for sale. However, there are concerns that I have when it comes to self-publishing. Mainly because the fact that nearly anyone can do it nowadays, and it has tainted the practice, especially when someone puts out a book that isn't well written or edited. There are fantastic authors who have self-published, and I self-published this eBook, so I am obviously open to the idea.

Should You Self-Publish? When it comes to self-publishing, there are a few things you need to do in order to be taken seriously and be respected. I cannot stress this enough; *please find an editor.* An editor is another set of eyes on your work and can fix mistakes in your manuscript that you may have missed if you edited it yourself. The editor can be a friend, colleague, or someone you paid. You can also have more than one. I tend to show my work to my writing friends before paying an editor to go over it professionally. I like to use a paid editor because that is their job. They are providing a service where I expect a certain level of results.

Nothing will hold a reader back from buying your book more than seeing grammatical errors in the visible parts of your book, which is usually the back cover and the preview. I've seen numerous authors just put out their work that hasn't been edited. It is not fair to your reader as well if they are correcting your grammar while they're trying to enjoy your book. Also, grammar essentially tells the reader how to read and interpret your words. If the grammar is bad, your message probably won't be interpreted the way that you wanted it to be read. It also makes you look like you're not educated.

The next thing to look into when it comes to self-publishing is the cover art. Your cover will be selling your book. At various conventions, I've listened to authors swear by having a realistic cover, while others will vouch for the free cover designs online. Honestly, go for what you feel will sell your book, and get input from friends and family as well. They will give you their honest feedback because they want to see you succeed.

You also have more control over the pricing of your book when you self-publish, unless you go with one of the larger self-publishing companies. Whether you decide to go that route is, again, a personal choice. Some of these companies will offer great packages you can use for publicity that will help get the word out. If you're planning on making appearances at conventions and book clubs, promotional materials are exceptionally helpful in getting the general public to remember you.

Should You Try to Get Published? This is a personal question for yourself. As I stated earlier, I feel there is a level of credibility when someone is published. You also have the support of an editor who will not only give you honest feedback, but will also work with a team to ensure that your book is marketable. You'll also have the support of having your book edited by professionals. The only drawback of being published is that sometimes your work will come out a year later, so there's a lot of waiting.

On the note of seeking a publisher, I have also been asked as to whether to seek out an agent. For my first published book, I didn't have an agent, but instead, I had a connection to the publisher who thought I could provide something substantial to the company. I highly recommend joining author circles and online groups, because you never know who is a member and who might be seeking out new talent. The more successful you become, you may want to look into an agent to help keep your best interests in mind as well as advocate for you in negotiations.

Whichever road you decide to take, whether it's being published or putting out the work yourself, follow your heart. It may sound cheesy, but it's very true. You know your work the best, and you know how to put it out there with integrity without the authenticity of your work being compromised. Whatever path you take, be true to yourself.

Also, when it comes to going public, be ready to respond (or ignore) to any feedback, criticism, or anything else that may come your way as you write. One of the ways that I went public with my work was blogging about my research topics for school. You won't believe what people will search for on the Internet nowadays, and there's a good chance that if you blog about your school work, or something about your day, someone will find it. While I've been blessed with generally positive responses to my blogs, you will have the occasional person who will criticize your work and call it poor. It is up to you on whether you want to pay attention to them. Naysayers will only have as much power as you give them. If the critic has a good point in regards to your work, then by all means, take the advice if it will help you.

Going public with your writing is a major step in your writing career. There is also a plethora of different venues you can take to upload your academic and professional work for people to review. In fact, I started uploading my old papers onto these websites so that I could get my professional work out there in cyber space. You never know who is paying attention.

Probably one of the most beautiful things about going public is finding like-minded people who agree with you and seek the same answers as you do. It's the quickest way to build a support system of colleagues and friends. Or, even better, your work will inspire someone else, or help them out of a dark time in their life. When we go public with our writing, we are extending a part of ourselves out to the world.

STAYING RELEVENT

Finally, when it comes to our writing careers, whether we are making a living or not, we need to stay relevant. This not only means writing something that is of interest to the general public, but also writing material that is relevant to ourselves. If we reach a point in our writing where we are no longer interested in what we do, let alone write, it is time for a change. Words flow the easiest when we are inspired and have ideas in our head. If we are not able to achieve that, then something needs to be done and it needs to change. If you're writing for school, while there is little-to-no wiggle room when it comes to topic, you have control over the content. Sometimes it's a matter of tricking your brain into thinking you are indeed passionate about the assignment.

If our voice is no longer relevant, there is no reason to continue writing. Somewhere, whether it is to ourselves, our friends, or our family, we are relevant. Someone out there is interested in our opinion in politics, business, the arts, and almost any topic in the world. To stay relevant is to remain passionate about what you do. As long as you are reading books such as these and yearning to improve your writing, you are relevant. Those who are constantly striving for improvement and change tend to remain fresh in the market, regardless of whether it is the public eye or the private academic institution.

Another way to stay relevant and on top of your writing game is to read the work and opinions of others. While it may be appealing to stay within your own writing bubble, it is beneficial to read the words of others. If you are striving to break into journalism, then you need to be reading different news outlets each day. You're doing this not only to stay on top of the current events in the world, but you're also studying style and structure. You're looking into the background of some of the most well-known writers to see what kind of path they took to success. If you wish to work in creative writing, then you're going to want to study different novels. You're going to be analyzing story structure, character, diction, plot, and more.

If you want to improve your writing, essentially what I want you to get from this chapter is to study. Look at the work of others who are more successful than you. Even mainstream celebrities have been able to write articles and books. While they have the support of an editing staff, they are still able to put their thoughts into words for the world to see. There are a decent amount of careers when it comes to writing. You can write for a pop culture website, you can become an editor, transcriber, translator, and more. Writing has become a lucrative career for millions of people, and there is no reason why you should be left out.

Writing will always be a relevant area of interest for the general public. If someone can read, then they can stay informed on the world news, and they can be taken away into a fantasy world where they can forget their everyday lives. Reading and writing go hand-in-hand. We can form the words all we want, but if the audience can't read, well, then it is a fruitless endeavor.

The art of writing seems to be both dying and blossoming. If you look at the writings of the late 19th century and early 20th century, you will find their writing is exquisite. The choice of language they use to describe their lives is like taking a paintbrush and creating art out of a mysterious landscape. You don't see a lot of that writing in the mainstream media anymore. When it comes to fiction, then yes, we might see this beautiful writing, but typically, we don't see it anymore. We don't even see handwritten notes or letters in the volumes that we used to. With as much information that is available to us at our fingertips, our words hold more power than ever. As the old saying goes, "The pen is mightier than the sword."

Words have immense power. They can start a war, break a heart, save a life, destroy a life, and tell a story. As long as we are passionate about our words, they will remain relevant. The time to improve your writing is now, and using books such as this will be a tool in your belt. Hopefully it will inspire you to strive for more in your writing life, and perhaps even turn it into a career. If nor, then hopefully your writing will lead you onto fruitful achievements in your academic and professional career.

So, when it comes to staying relevant, I want you to remain passionate. Don't let the stories of your life, or your opinions, fall to the wayside. Even if you decide to not put any of your work out there to the public, leave your writing where it can be found by your loved ones. Because after we pass on from this world, our words will remain. The most powerful way to stay relevant beyond our lifetime is to write, and to write often. The stories you tell in your journal or your laptop will give your family clues and hints about your life, and get to know a piece of yourself that never made it to the public eye.

Who knows, perhaps one day, in the distant future, your writing will be unearthed, and your writing will be the voice of our time. Researchers will study your words to learn about what life was like in our time. Think of the journals we have today. Do you feel that the soldiers, monarchs, peasants, etc. realized that their writing and their words would give the future the most reliable insight into a time that had long passed? Probably not, but we are now grateful that their words exist. Acknowledging the power of your words is probably the most life-changing step in your writing career.

CONCLUSION

If there is one piece of advice I want you to take away from this book, *I want you to write.* It may seem exceptionally basic, but just *write.* You won't see any improvement unless you apply yourself and just write. So often I hear from people who believe that they are not good writers. I don't believe that to be true by any stretch of the imagination. If anything, I believe that anyone can be a good writer, they just need to practice. The good writers are those who do it every day. With the rise of social media, people are now receiving an audience for their ramblings and posts, and this is the perfect time to fine tune your voice and make it heard.

If you are worried about the quality of your writing, perform the exercises in this book. Practice! You won't improve as a writer unless you're working every day beyond the school or work assignments. While it may seem easy, the hardest part of writing is the act of starting. With so many things in our self-conscious; telling us that we're not good enough, or smart enough, it can be easy to get frustrated and continue to write in fear like we are walking on eggshells. Eventually, you have to throw self-consciousness to the wayside if you want to become a successful writer. As you practice, picture your insecurities melting away with each stroke on the keyboard, or with each stroke of the pen.

Finally, I want to note that there is a support system out there for you in your writing career. It can be friends, fellow writers, and family members. I truly believe that everyone has a voice, an opinion, and a life experience that we can all learn and grow from. It is a part of the human experience. Writing is what makes us human and makes us care about others outside of ourselves, even if the person is fictional or not. As stated in the previous chapter, writing is connected to reading. As people need to develop a love for reading, we need to develop a love for writing. If we stop writing as a society, then the history of our human race may very well be eradicated in the future.

You never know how your story can affect another person. You never know how your opinion may change the heart and mind of an individual. As a member of the human society, *you are important*. Your writing is important. The more you do it, the better you become, and the better you can communicate the best of you. This is a journey that you are not alone in, and as the population of the writing world grows, we are taking each other's hand and bracing ourselves for the battle ahead that is life. The words that we write will be left behind as a testament to how we lived and experience life.

Write on, my dear readers. Write on!

ABOUT THE AUTHOR

Alex Matsuo is an actor, dramaturg, playwright by day, and a paranormal researcher by night. She is the author of *The Haunted Actor,* along with a book being released in the fall of 2015 based on her memoirs of acting and working in a haunted theatre in San Diego, CA. Alex received her Master of Arts in theatre arts from San Diego State University in 2011 and currently resides in Raleigh, North Carolina working as a teacher and podcaster. You can find more information about Alex at www.alexmatsuo.com.

www.ingramcontent.com/pod-product-compliance
Lightning Source LLC
Chambersburg PA
CBHW061801280526
45787CB00003BA/1440